Riding the Pennsy
To Ruin

A Wall Street Journal Chronicle
Of the Penn Central Debacle

Edited by Michael Gartner

Introduction

In 1968, two huge U.S. railroads, the Pennsylvania and the New York Central, combined into a behemoth that was supposed to help revolutionize the U.S. railroad system.

In 1970, the merged railroad went bust.

How did it happen? How did one of the largest corporations in America end up in bankruptcy court? How could any company lose $431 million in one year? And, equally important, how could this gigantic company go down without pulling a lot of other corporations down with it?

The Wall Street Journal, a unique newspaper that is the second largest daily in America, probed to find the answers to these questions. Its reporters laid bare the bickering between the Old Pennsy people and the old Central people. Its reporters pointed up the incredible confusion that had prevailed at the railroad ever since the merger. Its reporters discovered the inside story of why the government couldn't bail out the road.

The reporters turned up even more. They revealed that a group of officers of the Penn Central unloaded 40,000 of their shares in the road just before the line's travails became public knowledge. They discovered that a big and respected Philadelphia brokerage house, with close ties to the embattled road, led two lives in the weeks just before the Penn Central hit financial disaster.

They also delineate how the nation's banking system closed ranks when the crisis hit and helped avert further disasters. "The danger of widespread financial crisis and bankruptcies was very real," wrote Journal banking editor Charles N. Stabler.

While probing for the causes of the collapse, the Journal reporters came upon some unusual effects: The Penn Central debacle turned neighbor against neighbor on Philadelphia's fashionable Main Line, and it had ramifications at the Philadelphia Museum of Art and the University of Pennsylvania. Wall Street Journal reporters even found that the man who sold the railroad its red ink couldn't collect, and they located a panhandler whose take was off because of the bankruptcy proceedings.

The Journal started covering the Penn Central story closely as soon as its reporters discovered the line was in trouble—which was well before the railroad went into bankruptcy proceedings. Reporters in Philadelphia, Washington, New York and other cities have continued to probe and question and chronicle ever since.

This absorbing book contains a dozen or so of the more important stories the newspaper printed between June 1970, just before the line filed in bankruptcy court, and April 1971, when it announced the largest annual loss in the history of business. It is a chronicle of a classic case, the likes of which America had never seen in the past and isn't likely ever to see again in the future.

—MICHAEL GARTNER
Editor

Contents

Riding the Pennsy
To Ruin

The Road to Ruin

June 1970

THE biggest and most heralded merger in railroad history has turned into a disaster.

When the Pennsylvania and New York Central lines combined in 1968, the move was widely hailed as a step toward greater efficiency, reduced costs and improved freight and passenger service. Penn Central, the behemoth born of this marriage, was also seen as a base from which to build a huge and thriving conglomerate.

But things haven't worked out that way. Penn Central, the nation's largest railroad, with assets of close to $7 billion, is on the verge of collapse. Shippers and passengers are besieging the road with complaints. Anxious creditors are lining up, and most of the company's cash sources have dried up. Indeed, it's clear that only a massive infusion of hundreds of millions of dollars in bank loans—guaranteed by the federal government—can keep the railroad out of bankruptcy. And such an infusion is by no means assured.

Penn Central's woes have been apparent for months, but they came to a head recently when an obviously disgruntled group of outside directors assumed control of management. The directors summarily fired three of the top four officers—including Chairman Stuart T. Saunders, architect of the merger—and named Paul A. Gorman chief executive officer. An admitted novice in the railroad business, Mr. Gorman came to Penn Central only six months ago from the presidency of Western Electric Co.

The crisis at Penn Central has already cast a pall over other large rail mergers—such as the planned combination of the Norfolk & Western and Chesapeake & Ohio roads—still waiting for Interstate Commerce Commission approval. Critics are saying, rightly or wrongly, that big rail mergers won't work. One probable result of Penn Central's woes: Even further government control of an already highly regulated industry.

Where did Penn Central go wrong?

Fundamentally, its problems stem from the poor and continuously deteriorating service the railroad has provided its customers. That's the firm conclusion drawn from interviews with other railroad officials, industry analysts, shippers, regulatory officials and other sources. Their feelings range from disappointment to anger and bitterness over the merger's disastrous outcome.

According to shippers, Penn Central's service failures include every type of complaint ever registered, and in greater numbers than ever encountered on any other line. The list includes inability to furnish cars to shippers in sufficient numbers, lengthy delays, chronic jam-ups at terminals and connecting points with other railroads, misdirected cars and cars lost for weeks or months at a time. Major shippers even report examples of loaded cars leaving their plants only to return some weeks later still fully loaded.

"Penn Central's illness has been diagnosed to me as a massive case of constipation," says the president of one big railroad. "You can feed a lot of cars into their system, but nothing ever seems to come out."

H. J. Peters, director of traffic for Carling Brewing

Co. of Cleveland, describes the service improvement that was supposed to result from the merger as a "daydream." Penn Central's service today is the poorest he has seen in 35 years in the traffic management business, he asserts.

In hearings before the ICC, Mr. Peters described one recent attempt to ship beer from a Natick, Mass., brewery to a New York distributor: "Penn Central assigned three cars, figuring that each car could probably handle two shipments a month. But service was so bad, with round trips running three to five weeks, that the rail shipments had to be supplemented with truck shipments—and finally discontinued altogether. The distributor either had stale beer to sell or no beer at all."

Like Carling, many other shippers are diverting substantial tonnage from Penn Central to truckers. "If I can avoid using Penn Central under any circumstances, I am going to do it," growls Charles Sturgeon, general traffic manager of B. F. Goodrich Co. But because the railroad is so big and dominates rail transportation in much of the populous Northeast, thousands of customers have little choice but to suffer the line's bad service.

Penn Central's most publicized failings, however, have been in its passenger service. The line transports some 277,000 commuters daily in the New York, Philadelphia and Boston areas, using cars that often are 50 to 60 years old. Its passenger operations, including long-haul business, rolled up a $100 million deficit in 1969.

Public criticism is frequent and vocal. Pennsylvania Public Utility Commissioner James McGirr charged Penn Central with "a pattern of neglect bordering on contempt for the public," and he cited filthy

5

trains, decaying stations and poor maintenance. Penn Central concedes its passenger service has gone down-hill but says that the heavy deficits prevent it from keeping the trains in good shape.

Pinpointing the reasons for the collapse of the Penn Central service isn't easy. Part of the trouble stems from plain bad luck. The extent of inflation and tight money conditions in recent months hadn't been fully anticipated at the time of the merger in February 1968, Mr. Saunders told shareholders recently. Inflation alone, he reported, cost the company $100 million in 1969—$74 million in added wages and the rest in more costly supplies and higher interest rates.

Then, too, the 1969-70 winter was the worst in a century; this caused delays, breakdowns and substantially higher operating costs. Also, strikes in major industries cut into Penn Central's freight volume, as has the general economic slowdown.

Nevertheless, critics dump a lot of the blame for the company's predicament into the laps of Mr. Saunders and other top managers.

"The Penn Central board's action in ousting Mr. Saunders could be the most important development for the industry since the diesel engine," says one railroad executive, expressing a view shared by many.

A major obstacle to good management, insiders say, has been bickering between executive factions from the former Central and Pennsy lines. One former executive of the merged company recalls with disgust a meeting where there was a debate over whether to call the last car on a freight train a "caboose" (the Central's name) or a "cabin car" (the Pennsy's term). There were also arguments over such matters as the gauge (width) of track that should be laid, the former official recalls. Yet there was only a quarter-inch difference between the gauges of the two lines—an amount that has no effect on train operation.

Longstanding rivalries extended beyond minor issues, the former Penn Central officer adds. "It was a major management problem. You might have an enemy immediately ahead of you and a friend above him. It was layer after layer of a former Central man versus a former Pennsy man."

Even at the top, differences persisted between Mr. Saunders, who had been chairman of the Pennsy, and Alfred E. Perlman, former president of the Central and Penn Central's vice chairman until his recent dismissal. Mr. Saunders is a fast-talking, fast-acting Harvard Law graduate known to shoot from the hip. By contrast, Mr. Perlman, an engineering graduate of MIT, talks slowly and calmly and usually has a gentle disposition. Both men, however, have well-known tempers.

Insiders say Mr. Perlman was never enthusiastic about the merger—a feeling shared by his management team at the Central. ("This wasn't a merger—it was a take-over," Mr. Perlman conceded to friends after the two roads joined.) As a result, many topflight Central executives—including some key people from a marketing department considered to be one of the best in the industry—were lost to other roads. And if they didn't quit, they were often relegated to positions where they didn't get responsibility commensurate with ability, knowledgeable observers say.

Pennsy and Central officials had years to prepare for the merger. It was first proposed in 1957, though the merger application wasn't filed with the ICC until March 1962. Yet it's widely believed in the railroad industry that the two lines were poorly prepared when the merger finally came.

Frequently cited as an example of poor planning is the incompatibility of the Pennsy and Central computer systems. "There was no excuse for not designing the systems so they eventually could be meshed," says one industry executive. "The result has been total chaos in Penn Central's internal communications." When the computers failed to function properly, rolling stock and other badly needed equipment couldn't be located. At one time, an insider says, the merged company didn't even know its cash position.

Some regulatory officials and financial analysts make it clear they distrust statements made by Penn Central officials. For example, company officers had prepared financial plans indicating a first-quarter loss from railroad operations of about $50 million; in fact, the deficit was much larger. "Financial people don't know if Penn Central is deliberately deceiving them, or whether the company just doesn't know what it's doing," one observer says.

Some Penn Central directors feel this lack of credibility, whether or not it's intentional, has extended even into the board room. According to knowledgeable sources, some of the outside directors felt they had been "hoodwinked" by management after they picked up highly important financial information from a company debenture prospectus—information that hadn't been given to them as directors.

"The revelations (from the prospectus) were shocking," one source has said, asserting that they led directly to the ouster of Messrs. Saunders and Perlman along with David C. Bevan, chief financial officer. One nugget of information spelled out in the prospectus was that Penn Central had $41.3 million more in commercial paper maturing than it was able to reissue. In addition, some directors were shocked to read in the prospectus that first-quarter losses from railroad operations totaled $101.6 million. Penn Central had earlier announced, and apparently had informed directors, that the quarter's railroad deficit was $62.7 million. The announcement of the lower figure did not mention that it included income from securities and real estate held by Penn Central's railroad subsidiary.

—TODD E. FANDELL, JACK H. MORRIS, AND
JOHN D. WILLIAMS

The Roof Falls In

June 1970

PENN Central Co. has filed a bankruptcy petition covering its railroad subsidiary, Penn Central Transportation Co., operator of the nation's largest rail line.

Penn Central's directors emphasized that the petition relates solely to the railroad subsidiary and doesn't apply to the parent company or to the Pennsylvania Co., another subsidiary that manages Penn Central's extensive real estate interests, nor to the company's many other affiliated and subsidiary companies.

The petition was filed in Federal court in Philadelphia, and Judge C. William Kraft Jr. signed the order approving the petition. The action was taken under Section 77 of the Bankruptcy Act. Unlike some bankruptcy actions, which contemplate liquidation, this procedure provides for a reorganization of the company and continuance of its operations.

The court order permits the transportation company to retain possession of its properties, to continue operation of the railroad system and to conduct other business, pending the appointment of trustees by the court. The trustees must be approved by the Interstate Commerce Commission.

Directors of the Penn Central said the action was taken "because of a severe cash squeeze" and inability to acquire additional working capital.

The Penn Central's cash crisis stems largely from

the government's refusal to guarantee massive loan aid for the troubled concern. The administration had abandoned its plan to guarantee $200 million of bank loans to Penn Central after it became apparent that Congress wouldn't approve a proposed $750 million emergency railroad assistance bill if the loan guarantee went through.

Without the legislation, which would permit further assistance to the Penn Central and other roads, the $200 million wouldn't have been enough, it was believed. "We didn't see that there was any point in just prolonging the agony," one Transportation Department official said.

After an emergency conference in Washington, at which Penn Central's directors sought to get congressional leaders to reverse the decision, the executives returned to Philadelphia and began drafting the bankruptcy petition for the railroad subsidiary. This subsidiary has been the principal drain on the deficit-plagued company, going into the red by some $121 million in 1969.

The Nixon administration made a last-ditch attempt to get Congress to move quickly on the emergency assistance legislation in order to head off the bankruptcy petition, but apparently this attempt failed. It was hoped congressional leaders would accelerate action on the measure. The Penn Central reportedly held up court action on the reorganization to see if this move would succeed.

Well-placed sources doubted the Penn Central had any alternative than to file for bankruptcy. "If the Pennsy didn't file for bankruptcy, one of its creditors would have," said one large stockholder in the company. He noted that about $75 million of Penn Central commercial paper comes due shortly. There also have been unsubstantiated reports that $20 million in notes that matured recently are still unpaid by the Penn Central.

As of Dec. 31, 1969, the company had long-term corporate debt of $2.6 billion, of which more than $106 million was due in 1970.

The Penn Central's plight became starkly clear when the company called off a proposed $100 million financing in late May because it wasn't able to find buyers despite a coupon rate of more than 10%. Several days later, it became known that the Penn Central had used working capital to retire $20 million of bonds that fell due in early June.

Filing for court protection should relieve the Penn Central, at least temporarily, of a tremendous burden in terms of loan repayments and debt service. The latter cost the Penn Central more than $130 million alone in 1969.

Penn Central officials were bitter about the refusal of congressional leaders to cooperate in providing financing for the Penn Central and other financially troubled railroads. "They just don't seem to understand what's at stake," said one source close to the company. "That $200 million may sound expensive, but it's going to wind up costing everybody a lot more if Penn Central doesn't get some help soon."

It's understood that the Penn Central's cash needs will be at least $500 million before the end of 1971. The first $200 million, if it had been approved by the Pentagon, would have covered cash needs primarily for the summer of 1970. In addition, the banking syndicate that had expressed willingness to put up the $200 million if Defense Department backing had been obtained was understood to have agreed to extend the due dates on much of Penn Central's existing debt another two years.

The filing of a Section 77 petition doesn't mean an automatic easing of the railroad's day-to-day problems of operation and paying its bills. One Penn Central insider speculated that it may take at least a month for the court to appoint trustees who can issue trustee certificates, which have prior claim over any other debt instruments. Until then, it's doubtful that the railroad can raise any new money.

In the meantime, the source said, "the railroad just has to pray that people will pay their bills promptly."

The railroad normally collects about $6 million a day in freight bills. But as the economy has slowed down, this figure has diminished as shippers have stretched their payments out.

It is understood that the Penn Central railroad doesn't plan to pay its interline charges with other railroads that fall due shortly. It wasn't immediately clear what the amount of these charges would be, although the Penn Central expects to have $20 million more of interline charges coming into it than it would have to pay out.

An added problem may be that shippers, wary of Penn Central's plight, may try to divert traffic away from the road, thus crimping even more its much needed revenue.

Nixon administration officials, although bowing to congressional pressure in turning down the loan guarantee, are known to be apprehensive about the consequences of their action, particularly its impact on the financial community.

"We'll just have to wait and see," one official said.

He added that while big banks aren't in danger of being seriously injured, there may be "serious repercussions" in the commercial paper market. One government authority cautioned that this "object lesson" might make it especially difficult for railroads and other transportation companies to raise funds through such short-term notes in the future.

Eugene F. Schenk, president of the National Credit Office of Dun & Bradstreet Inc., said that he expects the commercial paper market to "tighten up real tight" for a few days as a result of the Penn Central experience and then return to normal. "After all there's at least $39 billion of commercial paper outstanding at the moment, and Penn Central's obligations represent only a minute fraction of this amount."

Commercial paper is short-term corporate notes of 15 days to nine months maturity.

Concerning the stock market reaction to the Penn Central's new difficulties, administration sources were hopeful that the repercussions might be less intense than originally feared because the financial community already has somewhat discounted the ultimate outcome.

Despite the guarded hopes for market calm expressed in Washington, sources closer to Wall Street were wary. "I wish I were out of the market," said one financial analyst who thinks the bankruptcy announcement "is bound to shake investor confidence."

He contended the action points up what he described as "the nation's liquidity crisis—both at the banking system and in the real estate market." The disturbing factors, he says, are the banks' failure to tide over a negative cash flow company even though its assets greatly exceed its liabilities and the inability of

15

Penn Central to "bail out" its transportation subsidiary through the sale of a few pieces of its vast real estate portfolio.

Because of the dismal picture shown by the Penn Central's financial statements, it'll be "touch and go" as to whether the road can be straightened out even under reorganization, a Transportation Department official said. While the road could keep operating, it is questionable as to how well it can provide services and whether it can make the necessary moves to improve its financial structure, he said.

Most officials of other railroads, while extremely concerned about the Penn Central's financial health, are hopeful that a reorganization will improve the road's operational problems. Said one official, "Operationally, the situation couldn't be any worse than it is now. The problems of exchanging traffic with Penn Central at our connections are so extreme that I don't believe putting the Penn Central through the bankruptcy wringer would hurt. And it might help."

Another high ranking executive of a Western railroad said, "After all, the trains will keep on running and with the fresh start they could get under bankruptcy protection they may have a better chance of solving their problems."

The government decision to turn down the Penn Central request for loan guarantees, while a stunning blow to the railroad, was a major victory for a loosely organized band of Democratic Congressmen led by Chairman Patman (D., Texas) of the House Banking Committee.

Rep. Patman had four principal objections to the administration's plan. He didn't believe the arrangement constituted a lawful use of the Defense Production Act of 1950, under which the loans would be guaranteed, maintaining the act was intended to assist small defense contractors. Also, Mr. Patman argued that it wasn't proper for the federal government to try to "bail out" particular private companies that happened to be in financial trouble, that there was "a good chance" the government would lose the $200 million it was planning to guarantee, and, finally, that the plan would set a precedent under which a host of other companies would come to Washington asking for similar help.

Although it will be too late for the Penn Central, the Transportation Department said it will continue to press for passage of the emergency financing bill. It said it hopes during hearings on that measure that "Congress will become convinced of the necessity of providing the Secretary of Transportation with this tool for possible future use."

It's understood that administration officials had become increasingly uneasy over the reaction in Congress and elsewhere to the loan-guarantee plan. A sounding of congressional sentiment led them to decide to scrap it.

Administration men rather bitterly placed the blame for the effort's failure on partisan political opposition. If the Defense Department had gone ahead with guaranteeing the initial $200 million bank loans, one official surmised, the temptation to "leave us out on a limb" might well have become overwhelming to Congressional Democrats. They probably would have delayed the legislation to permit further guarantees long enough for the Penn Central to fail anyway, he reasoned, thus leaving the administration faced with a

17

wasteful $200 million budget outlay in a congressional election year.

At a meeting with Rep. Patman, Treasury Under Secretary Paul Volcker is said to have indicated that the administration's decision to abandon the rescue plan was firm and that it had been made partly because of fear of harmful political consequences. Mr. Volcker is said to have remarked that the charge was bound to be made that "we were bailing out our friends."

Indeed, the charge already had been heard, particularly from Pennsylvania Democrats in Congress who regard the Penn Central as a long-standing political enemy—"a Republican railroad," as one of them recently put it.

As congressional opposition built up in recent weeks, it was evident that a growing number of Democrats from all sections of the country sensed political mileage in the idea of a Republican administration's willingness to use taxpayers' money to help the nation's largest railroad at a time when ordinary citizens are livid about rising taxes, prices and unemployment.

Opponents hadn't thought they had much chance of blocking the $200 million loan guarantee, because, coming under the Defense Production Act, it didn't require congressional action. But they knew that by objecting strongly enough to this procedure they could lay the groundwork for defeat of the proposed legislation to let the Transportation Department guarantee an additional $750 million in loans to troubled railroads.

The administration seemingly viewed the two propositions as inseparable, however. Convinced that $200 million wouldn't be sufficient to save Penn Central, officials expected that the company eventually would need a good chunk of the extra $750 million to be authorized by new legislation.

Thus, when the administration realized that the $750 million guarantee bill faced serious trouble in Congress, officials decided that the whole rescue effort was a useless and probably costly exercise that should be dropped.

Before meeting with Mr. Volcker, Mr. Patman met for nearly two hours on Capitol Hill with a five-man delegation from Penn Central that included Paul A. Gorman, president.

The officials showed Mr. Patman a number of documents he had been unable to obtain from the administration. These concerned the proposed loan agreement and the company's financial situation.

Company officials conceded to Mr. Patman that the government almost certainly would have lost the $200 million it was to have guaranteed, unless Congress quickly enacted followup legislation, it's understood.

One disagreement centered on the extent to which several banks are owed by Penn Central. The Banking Committee staff calculates that First National City Bank of New York, which was to have led the 70-bank consortium that would have lent the $200 million, has total Penn Central obligations of $396 million already. Company officials maintained that the railroad's debt to First National City was much less.

Administration officials certainly would have encountered a deluge of hostile questions from Mr. Patman and several of his Democratic colleagues at hearings scheduled on the legislation. The administration was approaching these hearings with growing unease, not only because of the committee's hostility but also because officials had been hoping to maintain as much secrecy as possible about the loan arrangements.

Several efforts were made to get Mr. Patman to drop his opposition, but these failed. In fact, Mr. Patman escalated the fight by securing an agreement from U.S. Comptroller General Elmer B. Staats to conduct a General Accounting Office investigation of the rescue operation and report back to the committee. The administration then announced it was giving up.

Under a Section 77 proceeding, the first action of the trustees is to determine the cash inflow and outgo so they can make decisions—subject to court approval —as to how best to keep the property performing.

The trustees can sell off certain assets as a means of raising funds and can issue trustee certificates—subject to approval of the court as well as the ICC. Such certificates stand at the top of the eventual creditor claim lineup. Falling below such paper are the securities outstanding in terms of their seniority. Equipment trust certificates likely would rank second to the trustee certificates in the eventual settlement of claims, followed by first mortgage bonds and other types of securities.

Final allocation of creditors' shares in a court-approved reorganization plan normally takes many years. For example, the New Haven Railroad entered bankruptcy proceedings on July 7, 1961, and there still hasn't been a distribution to bondholders and other senior creditors, although the Penn Central was forced to acquire the New Haven on Jan. 1, 1969. The U.S. Supreme Court now has before it the long-debated question of how much the New Haven estate should receive from the Penn Central.

Currently, two other railroads are in reorganization

proceedings—the Central Railroad of New Jersey and the Boston & Maine Railroad. During the Depression, there were scores of railroads in reorganization.

The key immediate effect of the Penn Central's petition to the court is that it won't have to continue to pay off on securities of its many component railroads that make it the largest private railroad system in the world. Penn Central Transportation Co. owns, controls or leases about 65 different railroads for which it is responsible for paying interest rates on their securities as well as meeting their maturities when they come due.

For example, the $20 million debt issue that the Penn Central was forced to dig into its working capital to pay just a few weeks ago was a maturity of one of its small component railroads, not one of Penn Central Transportation Co. itself.

Although Penn Central is now relieved from its continuing emergency of meeting such debt, it still has a massive payroll to meet weekly. It has notified its more than 94,000 employes that it expects them to stay on the job and to continue to perform their usual duties.

According to one insider, one of the frightening developments that hastened the directors' decision to prepare the bankruptcy petition came when the railroad learned that the First National City Bank of New York, a major creditor, suddenly stopped honoring Penn Central Transportation checks.

According to a high source, after the papers for the reorganization petition were all drawn the company's executive committee went to Washington in a last-ditch attempt to dissuade Mr. Patman from holding up the government loan guarantee.

"Patman and his staff absolutely licked their

chops," one Penn Central man present at the meeting said. "It was a complete farce. Nobody lost their temper but Patman's staff was especially provocative. They kept saying over and over that all this was a result of the administration's failure to lower the cost of money. It was apparent they wanted to bring us down so that Patman would have a dramatic example in the next elections of how tight money affects things."

The Penn Central insider added: "What he doesn't seem to understand is that the $80 million of commercial paper that is coming due is not held by the banks that he seems to hate, but by various corporations and investment outfits. There may be some mutual funds drastically affected by this."

—JOHN S. COOPER

22

What Happened?

June 1970

HOW can a railroad with $4.6 billion in assets, including immense real estate holdings, go broke? How can it keep operating? What's the likely long-term solution to Penn Central's woes?

These are only a few of the complex questions arising from the decision by Penn Central Transportation Co., the nation's largest railroad, to seek help under the Federal Bankruptcy Act. That dramatic move came after an unsuccessful attempt to persuade the Nixon administration to guarantee $200 million in bank loans.

Railroad officials, Wall Street analysts and legal experts generally agree the ultimate solution for the troubled carrier will probably take years to work out. Many months of hearings, investigations—and probably a few lawsuits—lie ahead. Also impending is a dissection of the railroad's complex financial structure. This consists of an intricate web of securities, bonds and other debt, including obligations of more than 60 subsidiary railroads, leased lines and other affiliates.

But close examination of moves made by some of the nearly 40 other railroads that have turned to the bankruptcy laws for help over the years and talks with experts familiar with the complexities of railroad reorganization suggest some of the possible steps that might be taken to keep Penn Central going.

Among them: The carrier's huge real estate holdings could possibly be tapped to help out—but probably

23

only as part of a long-term plan and not as a stopgap measure. Also, suspension of property taxes and other payments could be permitted by the court to ease Penn Central's cash position and help it meet day-to-day expenses. Transfer of passenger service to some sort of public corporation would be yet another step to keep the road operating. Finally, the court could order a recapitalization, a sort of alchemy whereby certain bondholders and other creditors could salvage at least part of their investments by receiving securities of a new corporation.

Legal experts hasten to add that any final plan might include all, a few or none of these elements. "It would be foolish for anyone to predict what might happen," says James William Moore, a Yale University law professor and railroad bankruptcy expert. "There are just too many questions involved in a company this big."

One fuzzy legal point is whether the railroad's creditors can claim any part of the assets of Penn Central Co., the parent concern. In any event, the debate could turn out to be largely academic. The parent company's only tangible assets—other than the railroad—are a small oil refinery in Texas and a fuel oil distributor in New York.

The railroad, however, does have sizable assets in real estate. But it's equally uncertain whether it can tap these landholdings to ease the current pinch. The carrier owns some lucrative Manhattan properties, including the Waldorf-Astoria, Biltmore and Commodore hotels. And its subsidiary, Pennsylvania Co., has substantial real estate holdings in California, Texas, Georgia and Hawaii.

But many of these holdings, particularly the New

York City real estate, have been pledged as collateral for loans or have liens on them and would be difficult to sell. In addition, many attorneys say that selling the holdings now would be something of a fire sale: It could bring some short-term relief but in the long run it might not be worth it. One reason: In 1969 the major real estate holdings in Manhattan generated some $20.2 million in after-tax earnings, much of which, Penn Central says, went toward meeting railroad operating expenses.

Furthermore, lawyers point out any sale now would probably produce a flood of claims by creditors unhappy with the distribution of the proceeds. And attorneys note that, in any case, the Securities and Exchange Commission and the Interstate Commerce Commission both tend to frown on selling off substantial assets outside a formal plan of reorganization.

Penn Central occupies a unique position under the bankruptcy statute. It filed under what's called Section 77, which is quite distinct from other parts of the Bankruptcy Act that provide for straight bankruptcy, or liquidation. Section 77, specifically designed for railroads, is more closely akin to chapters 10 and 11, those sections that assume a company has at least the potential for profitable operations. Thus, lawyers say, it's incorrect to say Penn Central has "filed for bankruptcy."

Section 77 was originally established to bail out railroads that had the ability to make money from operations but that were burdened with too much debt. Historically, a railroad going into reorganization has reaped two benefits: First of all, debt payments are suspended, thus increasing cash flow, which is net income after taxes but before depreciation charges. And eventually, through a recapitalization, the overall fixed debt charges are usually cut substantially.

In the classic recapitalization case, court-appointed trustees determine the railroad's potential earnings, before fixed charges. Whatever this amount—say, for instance, it's $10 million—it's capitalized at 5%. Thus, in this instance, total capitalization for the new company would be $200 million.

Trustees then divide this up into new stock and debt so that fixed debt charges can be covered with enough left over to pay cash dividends on the stock. New stock is then issued to the holders of the old securities. In the first New Haven reorganization, which began in 1935 and lasted 12 years, capitalization was cut to $385 million from $489 million. Fixed charges dropped to $9.1 million from $17.6 million. To be sure, a recapitalization would undoubtedly leave at least some creditors unhappy with the size of their stake in the new company.

But even assuming a reduction in fixed debt payments, lawyers agree Penn Central trustees will likely have to take far more drastic steps to assure a profitable company after reorganization. A number of attorneys suggest the only way to get the railroad back on its feet is to eliminate its passenger service, which in 1969 ran up a loss of $104.8 million.

Penn Central officials have already said they would like to do this. In 1969 the carrier got ICC permission to discontinue 27 intercity passenger trains; it has petitioned the commission to discontinue 34 more trains on long-haul routes. The railroad is already negotiating with a number of Eastern states with an eye to takeover of its commuter lines by state transportation agencies. Under such an arrangement, Penn Central would

in most cases continue to operate the trains on a contract basis, but it would no longer be burdened with
equipment financing and other costs.

Conceivably, trustees might also consider cutting
down the number of leased lines Penn Central has, lawyers suggest. These account for some 10,600 miles of the
carrier's 20,500 miles of track. Bonds and other debts of
the leased lines, which include such old carriers as the
Battle Creek & Sturgis Railway Co. and the Elmira &
Williamsport RR. Co., amount to some $365 million.
Presumably, if any leased lines were disposed of, Penn
Central would continue to operate them on a contract
basis, free of long-term debt obligations.

Transportation Secretary John Volpe has told the
House Commerce Committee that there was no cer-
tainty that the railroad could continue to meet payrolls
for its 94,000 workers in coming weeks. The payroll runs
about $20 million a week, with some employes paid on
Tuesday, others on Thursday. One newspaper report
quoted Mr. Volpe as saying he had been informed that
the railroad had only $7 million in the bank on a Mon-
day to meet the $12 million Tuesday payout. The pay-
roll was reportedly met by drawing funds from subsidiaries and by using funds that came in Monday and
Tuesday.

In addition to payroll and administrative expenses,
the railroad is obliged to make payments on equipment
trust certificates and installment purchases of rolling
stock. Some $14.5 million trust certificates and $51.4
million in installment payments are due in 1970. These
agreements cover a substantial number of the road's
freight cars and locomotives. Since the equipment
would be subject to repossessing if payments aren't kept
up, few lawyers believe they would be suspended.

27

There are some payouts, however, that the court has ruled the railroad can make at its discretion. Among these are property taxes and interline payments to other railroads. The company hasn't decided yet whether to pay all or some of the taxes it owes. Some $1.5 million is due to the city of Philadelphia, where the railroad is headquartered. The city has threatened to withhold a $1.2 million commuter subsidy payment if the tax isn't paid.

The railroad is apparently refusing to pay substantial portions of its interline charges for May. These are payments made to other lines for their proportionate share of freight revenues on shipments carried over more than one railroad. Generally, most freight goes collect. The delivering carrier collects the entire freight bill, even though its share might be fractional. Near the end of the month, accounts are settled among all the carriers.

Burlington Northern has already asked the Federal court in Philadelphia to make the payments mandatory. Judge John P. Fullam has set a hearing on the matter. It's expected other carriers and interested creditors will attend as well.

—W. STEWART PINKERTON JR.

Main Line Blues

July 1970

A LOCAL bum stopped a local businessman in downtown Philadelphia the other day and requested a dime. "Haven't you heard?" replied the businessman, pointing to the Penn Central headquarters from which he had emerged. "We're all bankrupt in there." The businessman kept his dime, and the bum shuffled on.

Thus do the effects of the bankruptcy proceedings of the nation's biggest railroad spread through the nation's fourth largest city. Since the 1800s, the Pennsylvania Railroad has been the cornerstone of the Philadelphia economy and the road's owners and managers have been the city's social and civic leaders. The failure of the railroad comes not only as a financial jolt to many in the Philadelphia area but also as a psychological blow.

Institutions such as the Philadelphia Museum of Art have lost hundreds of thousands of dollars on their Penn Central investments. The University of Pennsylvania sold its 90,000 shares in May at a loss of more than $3 million. Friends and neighbors in exclusive Main Line suburbs aren't fighting in public, but there is said to be a definite chilling of relationships as the road's reorganization procedure divides these people into opposing stockholder, creditor and management camps.

The 10,000 or so area residents employed by the

road are finding life especially tough. Many expect to be laid off (the road has announced it will cut employment 10%). One of their mutual savings associations, which holds $16 million of their savings, has been closed for at least 30 days to prevent a possible run by savers. Those executives who spent heavily to exercise their options on Penn Central stock have taken a beating. Ousted chairman Stuart Saunders is said to have been especially hard hit in this way.

Some Penn Central employes are razzed ceaselessly by their neighbors. "As if it's not bad enough worrying if I'll get next week's pay check, I can't walk out in my backyard without my neighbors razzing me about working for a bankrupt railroad," says an employe who lives in suburban Cherry Hill, N.J. "One neighbor goes 'Whoooooo, whoooooo' whenever he sees me, and another has taken to calling me 'ding-a-ling.' "

So ingrained is the railroad in Philadelphia's life that Nathaniel Burt, author of "The Perennial Philadelphians," wrote that for years good children in Philadelphia "were taught to pray for the Republican Party, the Girard Trust (Bank) and the Pennsylvania Railroad."

Today some Philadelphians are praying that the road will pay its bills. In testimony in Federal court, C. S. Hill, Penn Central's treasurer, said the railroad owes about $222 million in current charges for supplies, services and utilities. If debt service charges, equipment rentals and salaries are thrown in, the railroad's liabilities total about $2.7 billion.

The railroad is so strapped for cash that it hasn't even paid for all the red ink it has been using. Martin Bayersdorfer, controller of an office supply firm called A. Pomerantz & Co., says Penn Central owes his firm

$210 for supplies that include "a quantity of red-ink ballpoint pens purchased since December."

Also unpaid for are the spiffy green uniforms Penn Central ticket agents have been wearing for the past two years. George Bendinger, president of Bendinger Brothers Inc., says he is still owed about $18,000 on the $40,000 contract and has no hopes for payment. "I wouldn't have been paid anything if I hadn't marched into their accounts payable office last year and demanded my money," he says. He says the loss will cut his estimated profit by about 20% this year and will force him to postpone at least until next year a profit-sharing plan he intended to start for his 100 employes.

It isn't known how many of the 125,464 stockholders of the parent Penn Central company live in the area, but the number is surely large. For the investors, life has been grim. The price of their Penn Central stock has declined to about $6 a share from a high of $86.50 hit shortly after the company was formed on Feb. 1, 1968, by a merger of the New York Central and the Pennsylvania railroads. Moreover, after the predecessor Pennsylvania Railroad had paid dividends for 123 consecutive years, the railroad stopped paying in November 1969.

Many individuals and institutions in the area have already sold their Penn Central stock at whopping losses. The Presbyterian-University of Pennsylvania Medical Center lost $220,000 when it sold its 5,000 shares at $13, a source says. The Philadelphia Museum of Art is understood to have lost $137,000.

Howard Butcher, a local broker and a member of a Philadelphia family that was in the city even before William Penn arrived in 1682, serves as an investment adviser to the medical center, the museum and the Uni-

31

versity of Pennsylvania, and it's known that these institutions had invested in Penn Central stock largely on his
advice. Mr. Butcher, a kindly, rumpled-looking man of
68, had had a good record of advising the institutions
until then and had helped them make much money. Mr.
Butcher was a director of the Pennsy from 1962 to 1968
and was largely responsible for the road's hiring of Mr.
Saunders in 1963. The broker had extreme confidence in
Mr. Saunders and his management team, and just a few
months before the bankruptcy filing Mr. Butcher was
recommending purchase of the stock at $29, saying it
could quintuple in value.

Mr. Butcher now says he was flabbergasted to learn
in a prospectus that the railroad operations had lost
$106 million in the first quarter of 1970 after losing $193
million in all 1969. He declines to say anything else
about his role, but his brother, W. W. Keen Butcher,
says their brokerage firm of Butcher & Sherrerd liqui-
dated all its holdings in Penn Central after the prospectus came out.

The firm also advised some customers to sell, and
Keen Butcher says his brother Howard sold the 147,830
shares he owned outright only after selling out his customers' holdings. It isn't known how much people lost
on the sales, but Howard Butcher was recommending
the stock when it was priced at $85 or so, and thus the
losses would be considerable for persons who bought
then. Howard Butcher himself began buying the stock
in 1959 at $10 to $15 a share, so his average loss on each
share was probably not too great.

Although Butcher & Sherrerd says it was not hurt
much by its sale of the stock—it, too, began buying at
low prices—the brokerage house has announced a 20%
cutback in personnel and other austerity measures that

32

will include the paring of some salaries. The firm maintains the cutback stems not from the Penn Central troubles but rather from low volume. Of course, one reason Philadelphians might be leery of the market these days is because of the collapse of the Penn Central. Keen Butcher admits that "some of our customers have been a little restive lately because of our Penn Central dealing."

Some stockholders have decided to hang onto their Penn Central shares. International Utilities, the largest single stockholder of the Penn Central with 500,000 shares, has no present plans to sell the stock, a spokesman says, but the company said it would set up a $3.5 million reserve against possible securities losses.

Another holder who apparently hasn't sold is Mr. Saunders, the rotund lawyer who has been ousted as the $236,972-a-year chairman of Penn Central. Mr. Saunders won't comment on his personal affairs, but sources say he borrowed heavily to buy Penn Central stock at option prices far above recent quotes. Proxy statements indicate he spent $1,081,350 to buy 47,100 shares between 1964 and 1969. It is believed he still holds most of this stock.

Mr. Saunders himself has been even more secretive than the railroad he used to head. He is all but impossible to reach. His wife says she has been instructed to shield him from the press and not to reveal his whereabouts. Penn Central people helped spread an untrue story that he was in Europe. After his family was told that there were rumors that he was in dire financial condition, he promised to grant an interview. Later, he changed his mind and issued a statement saying merely, "no comment."

—JACK H. MORRIS

33

Bailing Out-I

July 1970

WHILE the nation's largest railroad plunged toward financial disaster in 1969 and early 1970, fifteen Penn Central executives took action that was to save them substantial sums as the company's stock price plummeted in succeeding months.

These corporate insiders unloaded more than 40,-000 of their Penn Central shares for an estimated total of more than $2 million. The prices received per share, mostly ranging between $40 and $70, were far above the stock's recent low of $5.62.

This insider selling occurred at a time when the investing public was only dimly aware, if at all, that the Penn Central Transportation Co. was in big trouble—which culminated in June 1970 in the company's decision to seek reorganization under the bankruptcy laws.

The Penn Central officers routinely filed prompt reports of their sales to the Securities and Exchange Commission, as required by law, but the transactions haven't been publicized.

Some of the sales took place just a few days before various corporate announcements that further depressed the stock's sliding price. But those executives who are willing to discuss their sales insist they sold for personal reasons and not because of inside knowledge of the railroad's worsening financial condition; executives' use of inside information to aid their stock dealings would violate the securities laws.

At any rate, the SEC is understood to be planning a broad study to determine whether any of the transactions might have been prompted by the executives' access to information ahead of the general public. The House Banking Committee, chaired by Democrat Wright Patman of Texas, also intends to examine insider-trading patterns as part of its investigation of banks' involvement in the railroad's collapse.

There is no evidence that the executive sellers did anything illegal. Several state that they sold because they were strapped for cash or because they were being pressured by banks to reduce outstanding personal loans secured by Penn Central shares, whose value dropped rather steadily for 24 months.

"The officers didn't know anything the public didn't know," declares William R. Gerstnecker, a vice president until September 1969. Mr. Gerstnecker, now vice chairman of Philadelphia's Provident National Bank, sold 4,000 Penn Central shares in January and February of 1969 and an additional 1,000 the following May 26—about two weeks after the company's annual meeting had heard a generally optimistic forecast of the railroad's future from Stuart Saunders, who was ousted in June 1970 as Penn Central chairman.

The SEC's Penn Central insider-trading file, standing more than a foot high, includes reports of transactions from nearly 100 corporate insiders, going back to the mid-1930s. The reports are made in compliance with a section of the 1934 Securities and Exchange Act that requires any officer, director, or 10%-owner of a company to notify the SEC of any transactions he makes in the stock.

An analysis of the reports filed in the past 24 months shows that Penn Central directors, with one notable exception, made little change in their holdings of the stock; most of the directors don't hold office in the company. In contrast, many of the company's officers were heavy sellers throughout 1969, and a few also reported major sales in late 1968 and in early 1970.

The reports of the 15 executives show only three purchases, totaling about 4,800 shares, in 1969. The purchases were made in February and March through the exercise of stock options at prices far below the market. Later in the year the three officers making these purchases sold a total of about 5,000 shares.

One director, David C. Bevan, who also was chairman of the Penn Central finance committee until the executive shake-up, evidently was the biggest of the insider sellers. In the first six months of 1969, according to the SEC reports, Mr. Bevan sold 15,000 shares, nearly halving his holdings.

He sold 3,000-share blocks on Jan. 6, March 11, April 9 and May 6. Additionally, he sold 700 shares on May 27 and 2,300 on June 25. Based on closing market prices on those days, his 15,000 shares presumably brought him about $840,000. The SEC file shows that Mr. Bevan's major acquisition of Pennsylvania Railroad stock occurred in November 1964, when he bought 20,-000 shares on options for an indicated total of about $420,000. (The Pennsylvania and New York Central railroads merged in 1968.)

Mr. Bevan, a director of Provident National Bank, isn't willing to discuss the transactions in much detail. "I sold the stock because my bank asked me to reduce my bank loan," he says, declining to identify the bank or specify the size of the loan. "I sold on a pattern and on the advice of counsel, when I didn't have any information that anyone else didn't have."

Besides Messrs. Bevan and Gerstnecker, the following were among major insider sellers in 1969 and 1970:

—Bayard H. Roberts, secretary, who sold 2,300 shares in a seven-month period beginning in mid-June 1969 for a total price of about $109,000.

—Theodore K. Warner Jr., vice president-accounting and taxes until May 1, 1970, who sold 4,000 shares in September 1969 for about $164,000.

—William A. Lashley, vice president-public relations and advertising, who sold 2,000 shares in March, April and May 1970 for about $34,000.

—Robert Haslett, vice president-investments, who sold 3,000 shares on July 15, 1969, for about $130,000.

—Guy W. Knight, senior vice president until October 1969, who sold 3,910 shares in July 1969 for about $195,000.

—John G. Patten, vice president-freight sales, who sold 1,430 shares in August 1969 for about $60,000.

—David E. Smucker, executive vice president until March 1970, who sold 3,600 shares in July 1969 for about $180,000.

(Messrs. Patten, Warner and Smucker are the three officials who reported Penn Central purchases in February and March of 1969. Mr. Patten bought in February the same number of shares he sold the following August; the other two men bought somewhat fewer shares than they subsequently sold.)

Other Penn Central executives who sold during the period include Henry W. Large, executive vice president until recently; Robert W. Minor, senior vice president-legal and public affairs; Jonathan O'Herron, vice president-finance until June 1970, when he succeeded Mr. Bevan as chief financial officer; Malcolm P. Richards, vice president-purchases and materials; P. D. Fox, vice president-administration until March 1969, and John E. Chubb, vice president-Baltimore. Some of these men sold as little as 500 shares, it should be noted, and several of the 15 executives still hold substantial amounts of Penn Central stock.

In retrospect, the railroad's fortunes can be seen to have steadily declined throughout 1969, but it's doubtful that this was clearly evident to the investing public at the time. Probably it was only after dividend payments were halted in November 1969, breaking a 123-year tradition, and after the company had to withdraw a proposed $100 million debenture offering in May 1970 that the gravity of Penn Central's financial troubles became widely apparent to ordinary investors.

Whether the company's executives could see, well in advance of the general public, that the railroad was headed for a crackup is difficult to determine; they generally deny that they could. All the same, the SEC records reflect several insider sales that appear to have occurred at propitious moments.

Four of the 15 insiders—Messrs. Knight, Haslett, Smucker, and Roberts—sold shares in July 1969, prior to the July 28 announcement that the railroad had suffered an $8.2 million loss in the second quarter, in contrast to a $2 million gain in the year-earlier period.

Four other officers—Messrs. Large, Patten, Warner and Chubb—sold shares in the period between Aug. 27, 1969, when Penn Central directors picked Paul Gorman as the railroad's new president, and Sept. 22, 1969, when the company got around to announcing his appointment.

At the time of the announcement, a Penn Central spokesman explained that the delay had been to allow Mr. Gorman time to submit his resignation as president

39

of Western Electric Co. After the announcement, some institutional holders of the stock expressed disappointment over the railroad's failure to name as president a man with a strong railroad background. In the three trading days following the announcement, the stock's closing market price dropped to $36.25 a share from $38.

Mr. Lashley, the public relations vice president, sold 500 of his shares on April 15, 1970, a week before the company's April 22 announcement—in the form of a press release Mr. Lashley recalls having helped prepare—that the railroad had suffered a $62.7 million loss in 1970's first quarter, compared with a year-earlier loss of $12.8 million.

Mr. Lashley says he cannot remember the date when he was informed of the first-quarter loss, but he is sure it wasn't far in advance of the announcement because "the financial types around here stay very tight-lipped." He declares that his only reason for selling the 500 shares—as well as 500 additional shares March 30, 1970, and another 1,000 the following May 22—was that he was under heavy pressure from banks to reduce loans secured by Penn Central shares.

He says that May 15, 1970, for example, he received a telegram from one of these banks stating: "Due to the stock market decline your collateral loan is under margin. Kindly make principal loan reduction of (a specific dollar amount, which he declines to state) or pledge additional collateral, or we will be forced to liquidate your collateral. Please comply by May 20."

Mr. Lashley says he never sold any of his shares on the basis of inside information, but he acknowledges that as the company's chief public relations officer he was exposed to a storm of rumors about the Penn Central's difficulties. At the time of his April 15 sale, he recalls, "I knew the company was having a rough time. I felt, in general, that there was going to be a loss" for the first quarter. "I had been getting calls from papers. By that time a lot of the Wall Street people were beginning to get uneasy about it."

The job duties of another seller, corporate secretary Roberts, put him in a ticklish position. One of his responsibilities is to supervise the preparation and mailing of the insider trading reports that Penn Central executives must file with the SEC. Thus, he acknowledges that when he began in mid-June of 1969 to sell 2,300 of his shares he was aware that many of his fellow executives had been heavily selling off their own holdings.

Mr. Roberts states, however, that this knowledge didn't influence his decision to sell. "I sold because I had to have the money," he says. He was faced with big family hospital bills, he recalls, and also was being pressured by a bank to pay off a loan. He says he told no one that he was selling his shares.

Mr. Roberts, who assumes "there is going to be some criticism" of the insider selling, believes the public should recognize that insiders who wish or need to reduce their holdings face "a hideous problem, a real dilemma" in choosing an appropriate time to sell.

Some of the other executive sellers aren't as interested in philosophizing about their transactions. Mr. Large, for example, briskly states that he "can't conceive" of anything unethical about his sales, which he says were made to pay off bank loans. He adds that a 200-share sale on Sept. 17, 1969, shortly before the belated announcement that Mr. Gorman had been named president, had "no connection" with the Gorman appointment. That's all he has to say.

Mr. Smucker, when questioned by a reporter about

his sales, replies: "It's not any of your business. I have no problem with the SEC, and I have no problem with you. Because I was an executive, my dealings were of public record. You have access to the record, and that's all I have to say."

A few of the sellers aren't available for comment. Among them is Mr. Patten. But his assistant, Charles Drake, suggests that someone "ought to write a story about us poor guys who were buying right to the end, because we had faith in this company."

—FRED L. ZIMMERMAN

Bailing Out-II

October 1970

THE big Philadelphia brokerage firm of Butcher & Sherrerd, known for its ties to Penn Central and its long-time advocacy of the company's stock, led two lives in the weeks just before the Penn Central railroad hit financial disaster in the summer of 1970.

Publicly, its widely publicized recommendations of Penn Central stock still stood. And in May 1970 the firm was listed as a member of the underwriting syndicate planning to help raise $100 million of capital for Pennsylvania Co., a subsidiary of the railroad.

But during the same month, well ahead of many investors, Butcher & Sherrerd quietly conducted a massive liquidation of hundreds of thousands of Penn Central shares in its customers' accounts. Among those unloading were members of the Butcher family.

By selling early in May, these investors were able to get around $18 a share, $5 a share more than was obtained by the far more numerous stockholders who didn't sell until at least two or three weeks later. By then the seriousness of the road's problems had become common knowledge and the stock's price had plunged. It eventually hit a low of $5.50 a share in August.

The firm's selling operation is noteworthy not just because of its size and advantageous timing. For years Butcher & Sherrerd has been closely identified with Penn Central. Howard Butcher III, the firm's senior partner, was a Pennsylvania Railroad director from

43

1962 until late 1968 and retained friendships on the post-merger Penn Central board. The brokerage firm's ties to Penn Central continued until just before the road filed under the bankruptcy laws through Butcher & Sherrerd's intention to participate in the debenture offering.

Whether Butcher & Sherrerd's customers benefited from this relationship isn't known; the firm's officers flatly deny that any sales ever were executed on the basis of "inside" knowledge.

But a reconstruction of events of May 1970, when Butcher & Sherrerd was selling the stock so heavily, indicates that the firm and other participants in the proposed debenture offering had access to crucial information ahead of the general public. This situation seems to have arisen partly because the press was slow in uncovering the news contained in a circular issued in connection with the offering. But the information gap also resulted from Penn Central's decision not to call attention to various important—and adverse—developments surrounding the proposed offering.

In most cases the company chose instead to leave the disclosure of news to First Boston Corp., which was to have been the managing underwriter. First Boston confined its disclosures to publication and distribution of the circular. No one ever issued a straightforward announcement focusing attention on important financial news buried in the 53-page circular.

Indeed, the month's biggest piece of Penn Central news—discovery that the debentures could not be sold—was never announced. It was implied, more than a week after the fact, in the company's three-sentence announcement that the offering was being postponed.

Butcher & Sherrerd's sell-off of more than 450,000

Penn Central shares in May—nearly all of them between May 8 and May 22—is only part of the remarkably heavy selling that occurred before the road's crackup. About 40,000 Penn Central shares were sold by 15 Penn Central executives in 1969 and early 1970. Several institutional investors also sold major blocks of Penn Central stock ahead of the general public.

The heavy selling is being widely studied in Washington by the Securities and Exchange Commission, the Interstate Commerce Commission and three congressional committees. An SEC official calls the study "the biggest reconstruction of a single stock's trading" in the SEC's history.

A major aim of the SEC inquiry, still months from completion, is to determine whether any shares were sold on the basis of "inside" information not available to the general public. Among the many items the SEC intends to study are the circumstances surrounding the abortive $100 million debenture offering in which Butcher & Sherrerd was involved.

It isn't illegal for a brokerage concern to execute transactions in a company's stock, as did Butcher & Sherrerd, while being publicly listed as a prospective underwriter for a financing involving the company or an affiliate. Federal securities laws would be violated, however, if such a firm initiated any sales on the basis of nonpublic information it obtained because of its involvement in the proposed underwriting.

That is generally what the SEC found to have occurred in 1966, when Merrill Lynch, Pierce, Fenner & Smith Inc. allegedly recommended that some of its big customers sell Douglas Aircraft Corp. stock because of nonpublic information Merrill Lynch had received as a prospective managing underwriter for a Douglas debenture issue. Merrill Lynch, without admitting the allegations, settled the case in late 1968 by consenting to the SEC findings and by accepting the imposition of penalties.

Butcher & Sherrerd officials deny there was any wrongdoing on their part. "I've been around long enough to know something about what the rules mean," says the 68-year-old Mr. Butcher. He says the heavy selling in May was based solely on the firm's analysis of public information, such as Penn Central's annual report for 1969, distributed March 26, and its dismal first-quarter financial statement, issued April 22.

Mr. Butcher declines to discuss May's events in much more detail. In fragmentary interviews extending over several days, he has variously explained that he's too busy to talk much, that he can't recall specific matters occurring that long ago and that he wishes to withhold public comment lest it be used against him by various investors who are suing executives of Penn Central and of Butcher & Sherrerd.

In July of 1970, following the road's financial collapse, the SEC sent questionnaires to more than 150 brokerage concerns, asking for details of every round-lot (100-share) transaction in Penn Central stock from April 1 through June 26. From Butcher & Sherrerd the agency obtained a computer run of all its Penn Central trades for the first six and a half months of 1970.

Most brokerage houses seem to have handled a roughly equal number of purchases and sales of Penn Central stock during the survey period. But Butcher & Sherrerd's Penn Central trading turned lopsided in early May.

From May 8 through May 22, the firm's records show Penn Central sales totaling more than 430,000 shares; purchases amounted to only about 5,000 shares. Included in the transactions in this period were sales of about 100,000 Penn Central shares—but no purchases —by various Butcher family accounts.

To help evaluate these and other sales, the SEC prepared an extensive chronology of events leading up to Penn Central Transportation Co.'s filing for reorganization under the bankruptcy laws on June 21. Comparing the timing of transactions with the dates of key corporate events is a basic SEC method for determining whether trades appear to have been based on nonpublic information.

In retrospect, it's clear that Penn Central was on a downhill run for many months before the crackup. Despite a stream of optimistic public statements by corporate officials, periodic financial statements grew increasingly bleak. In November of 1969 the company halted dividend payments, breaking a 123-year tradition. But doom wasn't clearly foreshadowed until the end of May 1970, when the proposed debenture offering fell through; that's why the heavy stock selling of the preceding weeks is drawing the SEC's interest.

Many of those involved in the abortive underwriting are reluctant to discuss it; one participant comments that "before we're through, this thing is going to be in litigation in nearly every court on the East Coast." But as pieced together from various sources, this is basically what happened:

Early in 1970 the company began planning a $100 million long-term debenture offering to provide badly needed working capital. First Boston Corp., as managing underwriter, says it distributed preliminary offering circulars to the financial community about April 27. The circulars contained new material about the com-

47

pany, but Penn Central didn't issue an announcement of that material, nor did it distribute these circulars publicly. Among other things, the circulars disclosed that Penn Central had lost $101.6 million on railway operations in the first three months of 1970; this distressing figure had not appeared in the company's regular financial report for the first quarter.

Butcher & Sherrerd says it notified First Boston April 28 that it wished to be included in the syndicate to handle the offering. Eventually, 81 other concerns were lined up as tentative participants. In early May, Penn Central supplied First Boston and the two other managing underwriters—Glore Forgan Staats Inc. and Salomon Brothers & Hutzler—with additional unfavorable information about the company's financial affairs. This led to the issuance on May 12 of a revised circular, disclosing the new material: The railroad's commercial paper (negotiable short-term debt) was maturing faster than new paper could be sold.

It could be argued that this was public information, but the company didn't announce it other than to supply it for inclusion in the revised circular. First Boston says that circular, unaccompanied by any notice calling attention to the material prompting the revision, was mailed out to the financial community plus a few publications on Friday, May 15. Later in the month a Penn Central press relations officer supplied about 10 copies to newsmen who requested them. The Wall Street Journal's report on the circular's disclosure about the commercial paper was printed May 27.

The revised circular named the 82 prospective underwriters, along with each one's tentative share of the offering. Butcher & Sherrerd was down for $850,000. Mr. Butcher recalls having received the revised circular

May 14, the day before it was mailed widely. Butcher & Sherrerd's sales force had already met May 12 and heard the firm's research partner, Edward Bromley, recommend the sale of Penn Central stock in customers' accounts. Mr. Butcher, who didn't attend, says Mr. Bromley recalls that his recommendation was based on his study of Penn Central's annual report for 1969 and on some operating figures just received from the ICC.

Mr. Butcher says he took the new circular home on the afternoon of May 15, a Friday, to read during the weekend. In an interview with the Philadelphia Evening Bulletin's J. A. Livingston shortly after the Penn Central's collapse, Mr. Butcher described his reaction on reading the circular.

He began reading with "great expectations," Mr. Livingston wrote. "Suddenly, as he tells it, he felt faint. A tabulation on page 19 showed that Penn Central had lost $193 million on railroad operations in 1969. Even worse, the loss in the first three months of 1970 came to more than $100 million.

"Butcher did some quick figuring. In the 12 months ended March 31, the loss on railway operations exceeded $250 million. Nonrailroad earnings couldn't offset that. He sensed bankruptcy, and became impatient for the opening of the New York Stock Exchange on Monday. He had made up his mind!"

Mr. Butcher twice affirmed the article's essential accuracy to The Wall Street Journal. But a few days ago a reporter showed him his firm's record of heavy sales before that weekend, including his wife's sales of 15,000 Penn Central shares on May 5, 7, 8 and 13; Mr. Butcher then described the Bulletin account as mainly just a dramatic story.

On May 19, in any case, Butcher & Sherrerd notified First Boston that it was pulling out of the syndicate. At the same time, other sources say, the syndicate was generally falling apart because of a growing awareness that the debentures couldn't be marketed.

Just as it failed to release other crucial news surrounding the proposed offering, Penn Central didn't announce the syndicate's breakup. Butcher & Sherrerd's customers continued their heavy selling, however. On May 20, for example, the firm executed sales of more than 25,000 shares, including 3,800 for Mr. Butcher himself. Total Penn Central purchases through Butcher & Sherrerd that day: 100 shares.

Sometime in mid-May, Penn Central played its final card: It began negotiating with Nixon administration officials for a government-guaranteed loan. These talks weren't announced either, apparently because of a rigid secrecy edict laid down by the administration. Whether word of the negotiations leaked to anyone in the financial community isn't known, but they did not become public knowledge until June 9; a government participant has since expressed surprise to a reporter that it took newspapers so long to learn of the negotiations.

At 1:15 p.m. on May 28, well over a week after the syndicate had fallen apart, the general public got its clearest inkling of approaching catastrophe. Penn Central issued its only press release of the month regarding the debentures.

"Penn Central Co. announced today the postponement of the sale of $100 million of Pennsylvania Co. debentures. Representatives of the company are working on alternate measures of financing.

"The offering had been scheduled for June 2 through a group of underwriters managed by the First

50

Boston Corp., Glore Forgan Staats Inc., and Salomon Brothers & Hutzler."

A reporter seeking more information was told by William A. Lashley, vice president-public relations: "We have nothing further to say."

On the day of this announcement, Penn Central stock was the fourth most actively traded on the New York Stock Exchange on volume of 188,200 shares. The following day it was third most active, with 191,600 shares traded. But by then sales by Butcher & Sherrerd's customers had slowed to a trickle. The firm executed sales totaling only 1,300 shares on May 28 and 2,-300 on May 29.

Mr. Butcher is vague about how it was determined in what order to take the firm's customers out of Penn Central stock. He simply states that when he decided it was time to sell Penn Central he began the long and tedious process of calling customers to recommend the sale. This took several days, he says. From the firm's records it appears that the heavy volume of selling began slacking off on May 25. Selling by members of the Butcher family occurred throughout the month, although nearly all of it was completed by May 22.

During May it was a rare Butcher & Sherrerd customer who was buying Penn Central rather than selling it, but there were some. One of them, Philadelphia lawyer Henry W. Balka, purchased 500 shares on May 25. He says that he initiated the purchase but that he did so mainly because of past Butcher & Sherrerd mailings he had received recommending Penn Central stock.

At the time of the purchase Mr. Balka held 500 Penn Central shares purchased through Butcher & Sherrerd the preceding November. "I called my broker and said I was considering buying either more Penn

Central or some Eaton, Yale & Towne," Mr. Balka recalls. "I asked him what he thought of buying Penn Central at the current price. He said he thought it would be a very good idea. He didn't tell me to buy it, but he positively didn't tell me not to buy it."

Now Mr. Balka owns 1,000 Penn Central shares. He was surprised to learn from a reporter that Butcher & Sherrerd had been liquidating Penn Central stock in May.

—FRED L. ZIMMERMAN

Pitching In

October 1970

"ON Sunday evening, June 21, 1970, at 5:35 p.m., a
group of bankers representing the major bank
creditors of the Penn Central Transportation Co. received the news that the company had decided to file
under Section 77 of the Federal bankruptcy law, after
learning that the government had decided to pull out
of its rescue mission. All of us knew that this tragic development would affect the financial affairs of many of
the major companies in the country."

So began a talk before the annual convention of the
American Bankers Association by Paul J. Hanna, a senior vice president of Manufacturers Hanover Trust Co.
of New York. It was one of a series of reports that together recounted a classic, textbook example of how the
nation's banking system functioned in a period of extreme peril, the liquidity squeeze of late June and July
1970.

Reflecting on the inside details of that emergency,
much in the manner of generals recalling a famous victory, bankers and officials of the Federal Reserve System provided a behind-the-scenes view of the dimen-
sions of the crisis and how financial disaster was
averted.

The discussions illustrated how the nation's seemingly fragile financial system, heavily dependent as it is
on public confidence, found the strength to face the
danger of a loss of that confidence. And the recollec-

53

tions also provided some lessons in debt management for banks and nonfinancial corporations alike.

The scene of the battle is well known. In an effort to reduce inflationary pressures in an overheated economy, Federal Reserve money managers had for months been restricting expansion of credit, mainly by reducing the lending ability of banks. But many corporations had found they could bypass the banks by issuing unsecured corporate promissory notes directly to lenders, usually other corporations, such as insurance companies or institutional investors. The notes—called commercial paper—were backed up, but only in part, by unused lines of bank credit.

The commercial paper market, designed for raising funds to meet current needs by top-rated corporations, was increasingly being used to free other funds to be used for long-term purposes, such as plant expansion. And as bank borrowing was restricted, the commercial paper market grew to tremendous proportions, reaching $39.6 billion in May 1970 from only $25.3 billion a year earlier.

Penn Central Transportation, the railroad operating unit of Penn Central Co., was one of many corporations raising funds in the commercial paper market. At one point, it had $120 million of paper outstanding.

And it was at this point that the company, which had other heavy debts and was running up mammoth operating losses, lost the confidence of lenders. It didn't have enough cash to pay off the maturing notes, and it couldn't sell new notes to roll over the debt. A bail-out effort involving loans from the federal government was launched, but despite early indications of success, it failed. At this time, the company had $82 million in paper still outstanding plus an unsecured debt of $59

million in Swiss francs, none of which had been backed
up by unused bank lines of credit, said Mr. Hanna, of
Manufacturers Hanover. It then filed for reorganization
under the bankruptcy laws.

It was too late to do much for Penn Central, but
now a broader threat loomed. If the nation's biggest
railroad, with a balance sheet showing tremendous assets, could lack cash, what about other issuers of commercial paper? Many had notes maturing, and the
paper couldn't be replaced by new notes if fear spread
through the commercial paper market. The danger of
widespread financial crisis and bankruptcies was very
real.

"There was calm in financial circles for several
days" after that Sunday night; it was "the lull before
the storm," recalled Mr. Hanna. But shortly afterward,
"finance committees and those in charge in placing
short-term money decided to reduce their risk by shift-
ing to Treasury bills and other high-grade forms of investment, as well as upgrading the quality of the paper
which they would buy. This meant that several companies were unable to issue commercial paper in sufficient
volume to match their maturities."

The banks responded quickly and, according to Mr.
Hanna, set up rescue programs valued at more than $2
billion in new credit commitments. George W. Mitchell,
a governor of the Federal Reserve Board, put the figure
at $2.5 billion, referring to bank credit demands from
borrowers who suddenly couldn't obtain credit in the
commercial paper market.

"I hope we proved we don't restrict our lending to
those who don't need us," said Mr. Hanna.

The rescue efforts took these forms:

—Additional bank lines of credit, some of them

from Canadian and European banks, with variable interest rates based on the current cost of funds borrowed by the banks.

—Sale of customers' outstanding instalment contracts.

—A special effort by insurance companies to buy commercial paper and support the market for certain companies.

The names of the companies that needed these emergency commitments weren't disclosed. However, one of them clearly was Chrysler Financial Corp., the financing subsidiary of Chrysler Corp., which shortly after the Penn Central debacle announced it had obtained additional lines of credit. There were others, said Mr. Hanna.

Major banks in the big cities provided most of the credit, but many banks throughout the country also were called on to participate. State-chartered banks in some cases were asked to assume a heavier burden than national banks because they can lend their legal limit to each of several related companies, while a national bank's combined loans to a group of affiliated companies can't exceed a single legally specified limit.

Meanwhile, the Federal Reserve was flooding the banking system with liquidity. "This event (the Penn Central situation) showed just how fragile confidence was and called for immediate, convincing action by the central bank," Mr. Mitchell said.

According to Donald C. Miller, senior vice president of Chicago's Continental Illinois Bank & Trust Co., in the four weeks following the Penn Central crisis Federal Reserve open market operations added over $1.2 billion to member-bank reserves. This was accomplished through purchases of government securities, which

56

adds to the reserves banks are required to hold idle against deposits. The Federal Reserve's purchases provided a much enlarged base upon which the banking system as a whole could meet increased requirements.

In addition, the Federal Reserve—which is the "lender of last resort"—assured the banks it stood ready to lend them emergency funds through its discount window. In the same four weeks mentioned above, member bank borrowings at the discount window rose about $500 million, again adding to bank lending power.

Finally, the Federal Reserve suspended interest rate ceilings on some short-term maturities of certificates of deposit. These CDs, which represent large deposits left with the banks for a specified period of time, had been declining as an important source of lendable funds.

In the months preceding the crisis, interest rates on competing money market investments had risen so high that the fixed CD ceiling had made this important source of bank funds uncompetitive. Suspending the ceilings allowed banks to raise immediately the rates they could pay, and funds that were flowing out of the commercial paper market were channeled into the banks.

In the crucial four-week period, while $3 billion was drained out of the commercial paper market, member banks ran up their CD holdings almost $4 billion, according to Mr. Miller.

Mr. Miller added: "This recitation of cold figures, however, doesn't adequately portray the nervousness or the psychological shift in investor attitude that occurred during this period."

—Charles N. Stabler

It's an Ill Wind...

July 1970

TO creditors, shareholders and bondholders of Penn Central Transportation Co., the railroad's decision to reorganize under the Federal Bankruptcy Act means plenty of uncertainty and woe. But for many members of the legal profession, it's nothing short of a bonanza.

Just how big a bonanza remains to be seen. But nearly everyone agrees the reorganization of Penn Central will be the most complex case of its kind ever to hit the courts. And it will require the services of platoons of attorneys, who will likely be toiling away for a couple of decades.

By the estimate of one attorney familiar with the intricacies of railroad reorganization, about 1,000 lawyers could eventually become involved, drawing fees totaling as much as $50 million. "And that," the lawyer adds, "could be a low figure."

Already, scores of lawyers are asking the U.S. District Court in Philadelphia for copies of papers filed in the case. "We've had about 20 requests a day ever since Penn Central filed," on June 21, 1970, says Phyllis Hunt, a harried clerk at the court. "They call from California, Illinois, everywhere. Besides those there are a dozen or so lawyers who just walk in every day and want the documents." Presumably, many of these attorneys already have—or hope to have—clients who may be creditors or who otherwise have an interest in the case.

Among other things, lawyers will be needed to represent the interests of the over 50 groups of bondholders of the railroad, its subsidiary carriers, leased lines and other affiliates. Major banks, including the 48 that lent the road $300 million in 1969, will need representation. Then there are countless other creditors, including suppliers of diesel fuel, wheels, track and other equipment, who will be pressing claims in the years ahead. Even commuter groups are seeking attorneys to represent their interests before the court.

Four major utilities have already hired outside counsel to demand payment of past-due electric bills. And lawyers representing other railroads, including Burlington Northern, Union Pacific and the Santa Fe attended a hearing in Philadelphia on the question of Penn Central's paying fees to other lines for use of their equipment and tracks.

So many lawyers clogged the courtroom for that hearing, in fact, that it was difficult to determine just how many railroads were represented. Most attorneys in attendance, while not openly exuberant, weren't exactly despondent either: Many joked, engaged in chit-chat and smiled a lot during the proceedings. "You sort of expected a wake," recalls an observer. "But it wasn't gloomy at all. It was more like a birth."

Another big group of lawyers will probably be representing many of the more than 15,000 communities Penn Central serves in 16 states. The railroad can cut off property tax payments during the reorganization and in most cases is understood to be doing so. Many of the communities depend on the payments to help support school systems.

Philadelphia attorneys are expected to benefit from a practice common in many courts that requires an out-of-town lawyer who wants to participate in a

60

case to have an associate who's a member of the local bar. For instance, when Burlington Northern appeared at the hearing on fees to other railroads, two attorneys were present: Louis A. Harris, a Burlington Northern lawyer from St. Paul, and Samuel B. Fortenbaugh Jr., from a Philadelphia firm.

Most of the city's big firms are expected to enter the case in one way or another. The 130-man firm of Morgan, Lewis & Bockius, for example, recently formed a team of two senior partners, one junior partner and two associates to handle Penn Central matters exclusively. (Morgan-Lewis already has its hands full as counsel for another financially troubled, old-line Philadelphia concern: Curtis Publishing Co. The firm is handling roughly 50 different pieces of litigation involving Curtis; over half of its staff is working on one or another of Curtis' woes.)

Two lawyers were among the four trustees named by the court to supervise Penn Central's reorganization. They were Jervis Langdon Jr., chairman and president of Chicago, Rock Island & Pacific Railway, and W. Willard Wirtz, former Secretary of Labor. Neither man, however, has practiced law in recent years. It's customary to include at least one lawyer among the trustees of railroads entering reorganization proceedings because of the tangled legal work involved.

Trustee salaries, which are set by the Interstate Commerce Commission, are drawn from the railroad's assets. When the New York, New Haven & Hartford Railroad began its reorganization in 1961, the ICC set the maximum annual outlay for salaries at $70,000 to be split among the three trustees. However, it's figured that trustees of the Penn Central—the nation's largest railroad—could earn as much as $125,000 a year apiece.

61

Trustees are, in turn, aided by their own legal counsel. Charles J. Milton, counsel to the trustee of Central Railroad of New Jersey, has collected some $90,000 in fees since 1967. Recently Mr. Milton submitted to the court some 70 pages of single-spaced documents detailing 1,481 hours of time he and two associates spent on the case from November 1968 through October 1969.

Entries include a two-hour luncheon in December 1968 with officials of the Reading Railroad, four and a half hours of work at home reviewing certain papers on the weekend of March 8, 1969, and 57 phone calls made in April 1969. Mr. Milton's statement has been sent to the ICC, which will determine his fee. Typically, a lawyer's time costs about $50 an hour. This would make the time Mr. Milton devoted to the Jersey Central worth about $74,000.

But some attorneys may have to wait quite a while to get their fees. One counsel to a bondholder group of the New Haven has yet to collect any money because the New Haven case is still tied up in the courts. His fee will come from the road's assets and will be based in part on the final valuation of the assets by the courts.

In any event, some lawyers could well make an entire career out of the Penn Central mess. The late Russell Dearmont was appointed counsel to the trustee of the Missouri Pacific shortly after it entered reorganization proceedings in 1934. The case dragged on until 1956. Soon afterward, Mr. Dearmont was named a vice president of the road. He moved up to president in 1957.

—W. STEWART PINKERTON JR.

Railroad Doctor

C AN the Penn Central be saved?

That question poses what may well be the toughest and most significant challenge in the history of American business. The answer isn't going to be produced from one man's efforts or those of just a handful of men. But if one key figure in the mammoth effort that lies ahead has emerged, it is Jervis B. Langdon Jr.

A tall, unassuming railroader with 35 years of experience in the industry, the 65-year-old Mr. Langdon is expected to be the leader of the four trustees who will administer the huge railroad while it undergoes reorganization under federal bankruptcy laws.

Mr. Langdon comes to the task without pretense of working any overnight solutions to the deep-seated ills of the railroad. He shares the widespread rail industry view that putting the Penn Central's pieces back together will be an enormous, if not impossible, undertaking.

But Mr. Langdon, who likely will have more to say about the railroad's future than anyone else, does have a plan. He intends initially to devote all his energies to restoring the railroad to the point where it can perform satisfactorily. If this can be accomplished—and many are skeptical—Penn Central will become a viable link in the national rail system, and financial success will follow, he believes.

"There's nothing more important to the future of

63

the railroad industry than making Penn Central work,"
Mr. Langdon declares.

Specifically, his plan includes:

—Substantial improvement in the dependability of
services provided to shippers, the road's bread-and-but-
ter customers, including a direct attack on Penn Central's notorious freight car shortage and record of poor
car utilization.

—A sharp upgrading of the quality of commuter
and intercity passenger service.

—Making Penn Central a dependable partner in the
interchange of traffic with other railroads.

—Improved relations with employes and government
regulators.

Any improvement at all will be cheered by employes
and customers. The merged road, formed in 1968 amid
great hopes and fanfare, has been a dismal disappointment in every way. There is a strong though not unanimous, feeling among those concerned that Mr. Langdon's choice as the key trustee was a fortunate one, that
he possesses the abilities that could help bring order out
of the chaos.

He comes to his job as Penn Central trustee having
already achieved a reputation as a doctor to sick railroads and as a candid critic of tradition-encrusted railroad managements. In the last decade he served as president of two major roads, first the Baltimore & Ohio and
then, for six years, the Chicago, Rock Island & Pacific.
Prior to that he spent 25 years in the legal side of rail-
roading.

Mr. Langdon, whose tortoise-shell glasses and
bushy gray eyebrows make him look like a fatherly col-
lege professor, is a unique brand of rail executive. At the
B&O and Rock Island, for example, he usually answered

his own phone and would think nothing of spending a half hour listening to the complaints of outraged shippers.

What's more, Mr. Langdon actually rides commuter trains—and says he enjoys doing it. By contrast, Stuart Saunders, who was ousted as chairman of Penn Central shortly before the bankruptcy filing, commuted to his Philadelphia office each day in a chauffered limousine even though his home was near Penn Central's main line.

Railroads typically are managed in a militaristic manner, following strict lines of command and rigid operating codes. Penn Central was noted for its adherence to this code, inherited from the predecessor Pennsylvania Railroad.

But Mr. Langdon's management style is just the opposite. "One of his basic objectives is to make everyone right down the line feel like he's a part of the decision-making process," says one Rock Island executive.

Not everyone in the rail industry feels Mr. Langdon is the best man to overhaul Penn Central. A few critics say he isn't the hard-nosed, tough type of manager that the road needs. "It's going to take some really drastic steps to save that line," says one rail official. "We all like Jervis very much, and he'll have good industry support, but I'm afraid he's too much of a compromiser to effect the abrupt changes that are necessary.

Such criticisms are rare within the industry, however.

There's little question that Mr. Langdon will be the strongest voice in the struggle to rehabilitate the railroad. To be sure, major policy decisions will be reached jointly by the four trustees acting as a team. But as the sole trustee with railroad management experience and an intimate knowledge of the industry, as well as the only trustee who will devote full time to the position, his views will carry the greatest weight. (The other trustees are George P. Baker, former dean of Harvard Business School; Richard C. Bond, retired president of John Wanamaker, the Philadelphia department store, and W. Willard Wirtz, a lawyer who was Secretary of Labor under Presidents Kennedy and Johnson.)

Mr. Langdon, who has resigned his Rock Island post, expects his compensation as a Penn Central trustee to be set at $100,000 annually, matching his salary with the Rock Island. According to tentative plans, the other three trustees expect to spend about 50% of their time—perhaps two or three days a week—on Penn Central affairs, receiving lesser salaries.

One of Mr. Langdon's first tasks will be to find a chief executive officer for Penn Central, who will report to the trustees.The man filling this post will be charged with straightening out the chaotic operations of the road and supervising the day-to-day business.

Mr. Langdon concedes the position of chief executive is a tough one to fill, presenting the most difficult recruiting problem he has ever had. "Some of the best operating people in this industry are scared to death of the job," he laments. "We can offer little more than the challenge of solving a problem that perhaps can't be solved."

Mr. Langdon's goal of maneuvering Penn Central into cooperating more with other lines in solving the problem of freight car shortages could be difficult to achieve. The shortage "is the most serious service failure on the part of the railroads," Mr. Langdon asserts, adding that Penn Central has been a major cause of the problem because its car ownership is substantially under its use of cars in the national fleet. Indeed, Penn Central often has 50% to 60% more cars on its lines than it actually owns.

Raising money to beef up its car fleet will, of course, be a difficult task for the railroad. One approach Mr. Langdon may advocate: a plan for industry ownership and operation of a freight car pool, with each individual road forced to make a proportionate contribution, perhaps with government aid.

Much of the deterioration in rail service has been due to the compulsion of railroad managements to produce earnings for shareholders, Mr. Langdon charges. The greater effort by railroads to satisfy stockholder demands at the expense of shipper and consumer needs has been self-defeating, leading only to still lower earnings, he declares.

Mr. Langdon says he isn't yet in position to judge whether Penn Central's diversification efforts hurt its rail operations, as some critics allege. However, he admits to having "wondered often how a railroad so terribly deficient in freight car ownership could justify spending all that money in acquiring Florida real estate." (A Penn Central subsidiary acquired two land development companies with extensive holdings in Florrida, Texas and California.)

While improving Penn Central's freight service is his prime objective, Mr. Langdon also hopes to do some good for disgruntled commuters and intercity passengers. On his first visit to Philadelphia, he says, he took a look at some of the road's commuter cars and found their condition "just perfectly awful." As long as the road has to operate passenger service, "I'll insist that we do the best damn job possible," he says, promising vigorous new efforts to insure that trains are clean, on time and manned by courteous crews.

While insisting on such standards, he isn't one to tolerate losses and low patronage from passenger operations for long. In his six years as chief executive of the Rock Island, the line, which once ran an extensive passenger service in several states, chopped out more than 90% of its intercity passenger operations. It no longer runs a single passenger train outside of Illinois.

If he so chose, Mr. Langdon could claim to be one of the earliest prophets of Penn Central's collapse, though it would be out-of-character for him to boast about his accurate prediction.

During the past two years he has voiced great concern over the continuous deterioration of the line. Over a year ago, when asked by the Interstate Commerce Commission for suggestions on the problem, he privately proposed a broad investigation into Penn Central's tangled operations and finances—a suggestion that obviously went unheeded.

—TODD E. FANDELL

Riding the Rails

March 1971

THE grizzled old Penn Central engineer peers from the cab of his diesel locomotive at the shattered windshield of a passenger train approaching from the opposite direction. The onrushing train has just fallen victim to a cinder block dropped from one of the two railroad overpasses in Lilly, Pa., a tiny Allegheny mining village.

"You know what's sad?" the engineer asks rhetorically. "The little boys who used to stand along here and wave at us now throw rocks."

The once-mighty Penn Central has indeed attracted a fair measure of scorn recently—and not just from little boys. Since the railroad subsidiary of Penn Central Co. entered bankruptcy proceedings in June of 1970, the brickbats have been coming from all sides. Creditors, stockholders, politicians, government investigators and the press have combined to lay bare a morass of potential conflicts of interest, questionable accounting practices, discredited corporate strategy and executive mischief.

But often forgotten is the fact that whatever else the Penn Central was doing, it was losing money hauling freight. And it still is.

To be sure, the railroad's trustees and new management have moved vigorously to improve service, streamline the company's cumbersome corporate structure and shore up its leaky finances. Damage claims have

69

been reduced, and customer complaints have dropped 75% in the past three months, the railroad asserts. So confident is the railroad that it's taking a number of full-page newspaper ads picturing its smiling new president, William H. Moore, with his cheery message that the "Penn Central is a revitalized railroad gathering momentum along the comeback trail."

That's undoubtedly true. But if impressions gained during a recent 504-mile trip by freight train through the industrial heart of Pennsylvania and Ohio accurately reflect the Penn Central's problems, there's little doubt that the route to recovery is going to be a rocky one.

SW6 is the kind of train the Penn Central likes to run. It's a through freight that daily hauls refrigerated cargo from East St. Louis to Harrisburg, Pa., a major distribution point for eastern markets. When everything goes according to schedule, SW6 makes the 856-mile run in 30 hours, stopping only three times to change crews and twice to pick up or drop off large blocks of cars.

But it doesn't always run on schedule—as is true the night I climb aboard the caboose at Columbus, Ohio. The train is already two hours late in reaching Columbus, and it's six hours behind schedule by the time it arrives at its next crew-change point just east of Pittsburgh.

Usually a 50 or 60-car train, SW6 this night is pulling 112 cars—95 loaded with everything from produce to pulpwood and 17 empties. The added length is partly the result of increased business, but it also underscores the Penn Central's chronic shortage of engines. The three locomotives on SW6 develop only about half the horsepower the railroad would like to assign to a train

70

this long, and the engines strain even to obtain the reduced speed of 40 miles an hour permitted during winter weather.

To make matters worse, J. J. Johnson, the conductor, laments that "it's been at least 10 years since we had good maintenance" on this heavily traveled route. Four times this night the crew receives "slow orders," reducing the speed to a crawl of 5 or 10 m.p.h. over weakened sections of track. From the rear platform of the caboose, Mr. Johnson points out the shadowy form of several crumpled boxcars, the remains of a derailment a few weeks earlier.

When the railroad plunged into bankruptcy proceedings, 2,103 miles, or about 10%, of its total track were covered by "slow orders," causing frustrating delays over much of the system. Winter weather has prevented much from being done to improve these conditions, but Mr. Moore and his new management team have devised a simple system for learning where the trouble spots lie. They have brought out of retirement eight office cars, or private coaches, which executives of the railroad use when traveling. "There had been too much track inspection from 35,000 feet," remarks one official in reference to the private jet used by the railroad's former management.

Efforts have begun to ease the shortage of locomotives. Late in 1970 the trustees arranged an unusual lease with General Motors Corp. to obtain 137 new diesels; they had been ordered prior to the bankruptcy proceedings, but work on them had stopped when the railroad ran out of funds. To pave the way for the transaction, five interconnecting railroads promised to buy 30% of the locomotives if Penn Central defaults on its lease.

71

To relieve an "almost desperate" shortage of freight cars, the trustees also have just won court approval to lease 1,000 new cars. The lack of rolling stock is evident on SW6, where only seven of its 112 cars bear Penn Central markings. The rest are owned by other lines and must be rented by the Penn Central at daily costs of about $3 each. Such rentals cost the Penn Central an estimated $47 million last year.

Waybills for SW6 show that shippers are being billed about $115,000 in freight charges on this train. But there will be little profit for the Penn Central. Besides car rentals, the Penn Central will have to remit much of the money to Western railroads in which the shipments originated. Another drain on Penn Central's revenue comes from the hefty terminal costs it sustains. Once SW6 reaches Harrisburg, the cars will be broken down and assigned to other trains for delivery throughout the East; some cars will be handled a half-dozen times or more before reaching their destination.

The new management is making strides to reduce terminal bottlenecks and is winning shipper approval for its efforts. "The Penn Central is giving better service now than it has in the past five years," says the traffic manager of a large Chester, Pa., manufacturer. An official of a Philadelphia container company, who once complained that the Penn Central took 12 days to deliver a car to a New York customer, says the attitude of Penn Central employes also has improved. "When they make a mistake now, they're eager to take steps to correct it," he says, recalling how quickly the railroad retrieved a carload of toilet paper that recently was misrouted to the company's siding.

But if terminal operations are improving, the Penn Central has made little headway winning changes in union work rules; the trustees charge that these rules continue to clog their payroll with 10,000 so-called featherbedders, or allegedly unnecessary workers. The Penn Central has been reducing employment by 5,000 persons a year, largely through attrition. The 90,100 persons it currently employs represent only a fraction of the 394,000 workers needed by the Pennsylvania and New York Central Railroads combined during the 1920s, the peak years of the steam railroad. (Surprisingly, only a third of the current employes work on the railroad as such; the rest are office and clerical help, computer operators and supervisors.)

The effect of the work rules on the hard-pressed railroad is illustrated this night by a westbound Harrisburg-to-Columbus freight that has been delayed by engine trouble at Mingo Junction, a crew-change point near Steubenville, Ohio. Its crewmen have already worked 10 hours; if they had continued to Columbus, they would have exceeded the 14-hour workday permitted by law. So the crew is flagging down a passenger train for the last leg of the trip, and a new crew from Mingo Junction is put on the freight.

That's just the beginning. Once at Columbus, the new crewmen will have to be returned immediately to Steubenville (by bus, if no trains are going that direction), although they will have worked only a few hours. If they are assigned to a returning train out of Columbus, all idle men on the Columbus roster—up to 90—will receive an extra four hours' pay.

Even working crewmen find there's little to do. Aboard the grubby caboose on SW6, conductor Johnson and his rear brakeman, W. E. Gordon, spend their nine hours drinking coffee, catnapping and discussing Mr. Johnson's recent vacation in England and Mr. Gordon's

Central's new Buckeye classification yard at Columbus. When finances collapsed last summer, he was ordered to dig up the rose bushes he had planted to brighten up his otherwise-drab facility. "My boss didn't think it was good for our image to have roses blooming when we were bankrupt," he muses.

—JACK H. MORRIS

On Top of Everything...

March 1971

REMEMBER all those bizarre stories about how the poor old Penn Central, armed with all that computer power and all those high-priced executives, was having trouble keeping track of its freight cars? How, occasionally, whole trains would be misrouted and boxcars would be lost for months, even years?

Well, according to an investigation now going on, it's likely that a lot of those missing cars weren't lost at all. They were stolen.

And that isn't all. As many as 277 freight cars, valued at more than $1 million, disappeared with the apparent help of what one source calls "well-placed" employes of the Penn Central itself. Many of the cars were then repainted, the serial numbers altered and the cars put back out on the tracks. In some cases, it's believed that the cars even moved back in use over the tracks of the Penn Central itself.

That's the picture that emerges from a supersecret investigation launched several months ago by the trustees of the transportaion company now in bankruptcy proceedings. The Penn Central is still treating the investigation as hush-hush. "It's the first I've heard of it," asserts a company public relations man. But some details have begun to emerge as the result of a search-and-seizure warrant excuted by FBI officials the other day in Chicago. A federal grand jury plans to begin in-

77

vestigating the case in Philadelphia, where Penn Central is headquartered.

The culprits in this latest version of The Great Train Robbery haven't been identified. It's known that the investigation so far centers on two obscure concerns: The LaSalle & Bureau County Railroad, an Illinois carrier that boasts only 15 miles of track but has inter-connections with four mainline railroads, including the Penn Central, and Diversified Properties Inc., a New Jersey company that leases some of the LS&BC's property for the purpose of rehabilitating or scrapping old rail cars.

The LS&BC, founded in 1890, is owned by about 30 members of the Carus family of LaSalle, a town of about 12,000 located 100 miles southwest of Chicago, according to records on file at the Illinois Commerce Commission. The Carus family also owns Carus Chemical Co., on whose property the pint-sized railroad has its offices. Indeed, the LS&BC apparently was set up mainly as a switching and siding concern to give Carus Chemical and several other LaSalle companies access to the outside world.

Diversified Properties is a bit more of a mystery. Its principal shareholder is Joseph C. Bonanno, a New Jersey businessman who says he isn't related to Joseph "Joe Bananas" Bonanno, a well-known Mafia chieftain who lives in Arizona. Diversified Properties' operations at the LaSalle site of the LS&BC are overseen by Anthony C. Crisafi, a Diversified Properties officer. Reached through his home at Essex Fells, N.J., Mr. Bonanno declined to comment on the investigations. A reporter seeking to question Mr. Crisafi at his LaSalle office was firmly ordered to leave. "You're keeping me

from doing a lot of work that I have to get done today,"
Mr. Crisafi said brusquely.

It can't be denied that things are popping in La-
Salle. A half dozen FBI agents, acting in cooperation
with the Penn Central, swooped down on the little railroad's yards, seizing the records of the LS&BC as well as
nearly 100 boxcars, some of them freshly painted with
LS&BC markings. Most of the cars were hauled off by
Penn Central locomotives that had been standing by for
the occasion. The Penn Central's tracks interchange
with those of the LS&BC about 10 miles outside of town.

Justice Department officials concede that not all
the cars are among those that were allegedly stolen. Diversified Properties holds a contract with Equitable Life
Assurance Society of the U.S. to take over 466 old cars
operated by the Penn Central under a leaseback arrangement with Equitable, which is one of the Penn
Central's biggest creditors.

A spokesman for Diversified Properties and Mr.
Bonanno said that the cars were being refurbished and
leased to the LS&BC, "which puts freight on them and
then ships them out."

Equitable officials acknowledge the contract and
say that Diversified Properties has performed satisfactorily under it.

But Louis C. Bechtle, U.S. attorney for the Philadelphia region, asserted in his announcement of the sei-
zures that an additional 277 Penn Central freight cars
"have been routed onto the tracks of the LaSalle & Bureau County and have disappeared, turning up grad-
ually with all Penn Central identity concealed. . . ."
And sources close to the case indicate there is a possibil-
ity that a similar fate met rail cars from at least one
other line, an unidentified major Western railroad.

Penn Central officials adamantly refuse to discuss details of the case except to emphasize that the alleged plot was uncovered through the railroad's own investigative efforts. But sources close to the situation offer the following scenario:

Penn Central employes, well aware of the chaos that has prevailed in the railroad's system before and after the financial collapse of the line, helped divert a steady stream of empty freight cars off the Penn Central tracks in early 1970. The cars, worth an average of about $4,000 (indicating they were probably 10 to 20 years old since new freight cars sell for $10,000 and up), were sent to three central switching yards and thence routed to the LaSalle & Bureau County tracks in Illinois.

The "cooperative" Penn Central employes haven't yet been identified, but it's understood statements have been taken from a number of them and subpoenas are expected to be issued in connection with the Grand Jury inquiry. One qualified source asserted flatly that "there is no question Penn Central people were involved in this."

Just what happened to the cars after they reached the LS&BC yards is a little hazy, too. "We haven't been able to trace all the missing cars," says one investigator. "We think some of them were scrapped—for about $1,000 a car—while others were fed back into the lines and put under new leases." According to an affidavit filed by the FBI with a federal court in Chicago, at least 11 of the cars—bearing the LS&BC seal but with their old Penn Central serial numbers intact—were found on the tracks of the Penn Central itself.

Officials of the LaSalle & Bureau County and Carus Chemical deny any wrongdoing. "First we heard about it was yesterday," says Herman Carus, a vice president

80

of the railroad. "Our people tell us it's just a goof. I don't read your paper to read about people who get into trouble because they goof. That's not American."

—Thomas J. Bray and Francis L. Partsch

A Final Irony

March 1971

A FTER years of waiting and watching, William Jermann, a professor of electrical engineering at Memphis State University, is on the threshold of achieving a long-sought investment goal—he has just placed an order for 100 shares of Penn Central Co. stock at $6 a share.

Penn Central stock? Sure, says Mr. Jermann, who doesn't see anything particularly puzzling about investing in a company whose only asset is in bankruptcy proceedings. Actually, it's rather simple, he explains. "When the Penn Central was a going concern, I couldn't afford to buy it."

Whatever the merit of such logic, Mr. Jermann isn't alone in his thinking. In the nine months since the Penn Central railroad went bust—with a thud that is still reverberating in the financial community—trading in shares of the parent has remained heavy. Volume on the New York Stock Exchange has averaged better than 30,000 shares a day—well above the volume of most Big Board shares—and on some days up to 100,000 shares have traded hands.

Indeed, so many people are clamoring for a piece of the Penn Central action that the company has had to order a new batch of stock certificates. Archibald deB. Johnson, the corporate secretary, adds that the company's list of shareholders has ballooned by some 20,000, to 145,000, since the bankruptcy proceedings of Penn

Central Transportation Co., the company's subsidiary, began in June 1970.

Where there's a buyer there must be a seller, and every indication is that in the case of the Penn Central the little man is rushing in while the big boys are rushing out. Mutual funds held only 369,000 of Penn Central's 24.1 million shares at the end of 1970, down from 1.5 million a year earlier, according to Vickers Associates, which keeps tabs on such things.

"I can think of a thousand reasons for selling, but not a one for buying," scoffs a broker who specializes in big, sophisticated institutional accounts.

It's possible, of course, that the big money will prove wrong. Penn Central's new management has made some impressive gains in improving service, and if they succeed in revitalizing the railroad people like William Jermann could profit handsomely. Anyone who bought at $5.50 a share immediately after the bankruptcy and sold at the high of $9.25 reached last fall has already turned a pretty penny.

But stock analysts who have followed the Penn Central for years are nearly unanimous in their belief that anyone planning to retire on his Penn Central stock had better be in diapers today. "The more sophisticated you are, the less value you can see in Penn Central," says one analyst. Comments another: "Those who buy must subscribe to the 'greater fool theory'—the belief that no matter what they get stuck with, there's bound to be someone else who'll pay more for it in the future."

The analysts claim solid ground for their pessimism. The railroad, they assert, is hopelessly insolvent. Losses are continuing, debt is mounting and there is a backlog of deferred maintenance that may approach $1 billion. In addition, Oscar Lasdon, a New York authority on railroad bankruptcies, notes that in all but two of the 57 railroad bankruptcy cases since the depression, common shareholders have had their equity totally wiped out in the lengthy reorganization procedures.

So why are people buying?

"People will buy anything if it's cheap enough," says Howard K. Butcher III, a Philadelphia broker and former Penn Central director who for years was a leading advocate of the company's stock. When the railroad's financial problems surfaced last May, Mr. Butcher reversed his long-standing (and now-controversial) "buy" recommendation for the stock and helped his firm, Butcher & Sherrerd, and its customers liquidate more than 450,000 Penn Central shares.

Some who sold are again buying and today hold more of "that stuff" than ever before, Mr. Butcher says. "I don't know why people buy it," the rumpled broker says. "I tell them it will be 10 years before the railroad can be reorganized. But there are some people who just can't get over the fact that they can buy for $6 to $7 today stock that recently sold for $85 a share. Why, I've got people who'd buy 10,000 to 20,000 shares if I just gave the OK."

Brokers across the country report a similar, albeit less spectacular, trend. "It isn't just the little lady in Keokuk who's buying," says a Chicago broker. "A lot of it's coming from wealthy businessmen who like to speculate, but who just haven't done their homework."

So long as all the facts on the railroad's problems are publicly available and a court hasn't ruled that there is no equity behind the shares, neither the New York Stock Exchange nor the Securities and Exchange Commission is likely to move to delist the Penn Central.

"It isn't the government's role to substitute its judgment for that of the investor on the value of a stock," an SEC lawyer says.

Besides, "there are a great many shares traded today that are of doubtful value," says Gaylord P. Harnwell, Penn Central Co. president. Significantly, however, he, William H. Moore, the president of the railroad, and the railroad's four trustees haven't purchased a share of stock in the company since the bankruptcy.

It is true, as those who are buying note, that only the railroad subsidiary, Penn Central Transportation Co., is in bankruptcy proceedings, while the parent Penn Central Co. remains solvent. But the difference is more technical than tangible. To avoid a lawsuit, directors of the parent company recently agreed to return two small oil companies to their former owners, reducing Penn Central's assets to its ownership of the transportation company. The company's much vaunted real estate, including its Manhattan hotels, are actually subsidiaries of the railroad and thus beyond the reach of Penn Central shareholders. In addition, nearly all the real estate is pledged against loans to the railroad.

Furthermore, to prevent the holders of $50 million in overdue Swiss franc notes from foreclosing, Penn Central directors have agreed to issue a new series of notes convertible into seven million shares, or a 29% interest, in the company's stock.

So broke is the parent company that it can't even afford office space for its two remaining employes. Mr. Johnson, the secretary, keeps a desk in the office of a contractors' trade association, while Mr. Harnwell, the president, maintains an office at the University of Pennsylvania, where he recently retired as president.

While analysts give high marks to the railroad's

new management, they remain skeptical that the trustees can achieve the "tough conditions" they say are necessary for survival. These include a drastic cut in service and an end to union featherbedding, for instance. But even if the staggering operating losses are stemmed, there's that mountain of maintenance work and debt to be overcome.

At the end of November 1970, the Penn Central had $129 million in long-term debt and $47.5 million in interest in default, and the figures are swelling at the rate of $17 million a month. As Mr. Lasdon, the bankruptcy expert, points out, "The longer these accruals are extended, the greater they become and the more remote become the chances that there will be any equity for the common stock."

What's more, the $100 million in government-backed trustees certificates sold earlier this year can't even be extended when they start coming due in five years, and they take precedence over all other creditor and stockholder claims.

Many of those who retain their Penn Central securities cling to the hope that the government will step in and buy the railroad—and at a premium price. But with such critics of the Penn Central as Wright Patman (D., Texas) and Vance Hartke (D., Ind.) in Congress, it's doubtful that shareholders would fare any better under nationalization than they would under reorganization, analysts contend.

Even Penn Central's potentially huge tax shelter appears more hopeful than real. F. Scott Nichols, an analyst with Moore & Schley, Cameron & Co. in New York believes that the tax benefits can be used only if a small and profitable fish swallows the dying Penn Central whale. And even then there would have to be a substantial dilution in the price of Penn Central's stock.

"It's one of the oddities of the Penn Central that its stock has always sold for much more than its worth," says Mr. Nichols. "When it was selling for $78 a share in April 1968, I thought it would be a good buy at $50. When it fell to $30, I saw it as a $15 stock. Today it might have some value as a tax loss at $2 a share."

There's always the long shot, however, as the St. Louis Southwestern Railway proved more than 20 years ago. In a case regarded more as a fluke today than as an example, the Cotton Belt Route went bankrupt in 1944, had its stock delisted as worthless—and then made money hand over fist. In fact, it was able to pay off its debts and win dismissal of its bankruptcy petition. When trading in the stock resumed in 1947, it opened at $60.25 a share, Mr. Lasdon recalls, and by 1951 shot up to $320 a share.

But as a porter at a Philadelphia station says, "It'll take a heap of baking powder before the Penn Central rises again."

—JACK H. MORRIS

Epilogue

Penn Central Transportation Co. reported that it suffered a $141.2 million loss during December, bringing its total loss for 1970 to a staggering $431.2 million.

Both the December and full-year figures are on a preliminary basis and include special write-offs totaling $101.5 million from a reduction in the railroad's track and the impairment of some of its investments.

The loss was far greater than had been publicly predicted by trustees of the Penn Central Co. unit, which is in reorganization proceedings. In testimony before a House Commerce subcommittee on March 9, for instance, Jervis Langdon Jr., one of the trustees, estimated the 1970 deficit to be $309.2 million.

Trustees said the figures are on a fully accrued basis and in accordance with reports to the Interstate Commerce Commission. On the same basis, the railroad lost $91.6 million in 1969.

However, on the basis of generally accepted accounting principles that Penn Central used in reporting its financial figures in 1969, the loss for that year amounted to $182.3 million, including a special $126 million writedown on the company's investment in long-haul passenger service west of Harrisburg, Pa., and Albany, N.Y.

The 1970 loss works out to $13.67 for each second of 1970.

According to the Guinness Book of World Records, the previous biggest loss was $143.2 million, posted by General Dynamics Corp. in 1961. General Dynamics, however, has since reduced its loss for that year to $69.4

89

million to reflect subsequent tax credits and other accounting changes.

The special Penn Central charges during 1970 include $42.4 million for the service value of some unnamed rail lines the trustees said were retired during 1970, and $14.2 million in costs related to dismantling those lines. In addition, the company said it wrote off the value of its investments by $44.9 million, principally its holdings in Lehigh Valley Railroad, which is also in reorganization proceedings. The figure includes a $17 million write-off made earlier in the year.

Freight revenue for December fell to $108.1 million from $122.2 million in the year-earlier month, but freight revenue increased to $1.39 billion from $1.34 billion for the full year, largely because of freight rate increases. Total operating revenue for the Penn Central rose to $1.69 billion from $1.65 billion in 1969.

Operating expenses also increased sharply, the trustees said, because of higher wage and material expenses.

The company said that its income from operations other than rail fell to $83.4 million from $119 million in 1969, chiefly because of the reduction in dividend income from its subsidiaries.

In what has now become a standard disclaimer, the trustees said comparison with 1969 figures would be "misleading since the prior figures appear to have reflected a corporate policy at that time of putting the best conceivable face on the facts."

Penn Central also has reported a loss of $66.3 million for the first two months of 1971, compared with a $73.1 million deficit for January and February 1970.

—JACK S. MORRIS